Wobbly Walruses

by Charles Rotter

sundance™

A Haights Cross Communications Company

Sundance/Newbridge Educational Publishing, LLC
One Beeman Road
P.O. Box 740
Northborough, MA 01532-0740
800-343-8204
www.sundancepub.com

Adapted from *Naturebooks,* published in 2001 by The Child's World®, Inc.
P.O. Box 326
Chanhassen, MN 55317-0326

Photo Credits: Front cover, p. 10 © Rod Planck/Dembinsky Photo
Assoc., Inc.; p. 2 © Dominique Braud/Dembinsky Photo Assoc., Inc.;
p. 6 © Harry M. Walker; pp. 9, 22 © Erwin and Peggy Bauer; p. 13
© Ingrid Visser/Ursus Photography; p. 14 © Carleton Ray, The National
Audubon Society Collection/Photo Researchers; p. 17 © Phil A. Dotson,
The National Audubon Society Collection/Photo Researchers; p. 21
© Francis Caldwell/Visuals Unlimited; p. 29 © Henry H. Holdsworth;
p. 30 © Richard Kolar/Animals Animals; back cover, pp. 18, 25, 26
© Paul Nicklen/Ursus Photography

ISBN 978-0-7608-9350-0

Printed in China

Contents

1 Meet the Walrus!

It is a sunny day in the **far north.**
Waves crash and splash against the shore.
Hundreds of big animals are **napping** on
the rocks. Each one has a small head and a
fat body. They do not have any arms or legs.
Instead, they have **short flippers.**
One of the animals moves to the edge of the
rock it is on. Then it dives into the water.

It's a **walrus!**

This large walrus is standing
in shallow water near
a beach in Alaska.

Walruses are **mammals.** This means that they have a warm body and can make milk for their babies. Walruses are also **pinnipeds.** Their body has flippers where land mammals have arms or legs. Seals and sea lions are also pinnipeds.

Walruses grow **large and heavy.** Some weigh more than 3,500 pounds! They have **thick, brown skin.** And they have small, round eyes. Walruses also have **tusks.** These teeth can grow up to three feet long.

This male walrus is resting on some rocks.

Walruses use their tusks in many ways. They **dig up food** with them. They use them to fight enemies. Tusks even help walruses get out of the water.

Walruses have almost no hair on their body. They have special hairs on their face, though. These hairs make the walrus look like it has **a mustache!** But these hairs are more like a cat's whiskers. A walrus uses them to find its way in dark water. It can also find food using them.

This walrus is digging into the dirt with its tusks to pull itself onto the shore.

3 Where Do Walruses Live?

Walruses spend a lot of time in the ocean. They live in **the Arctic,** where it is very cold. The ocean there is often covered with ice. But walruses *don't seem to mind* the cold. They come out of the water just to lie on top of the ice!

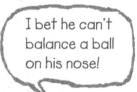

I bet he can't balance a ball on his nose!

This walrus is resting in the snow on a sunny afternoon.

Walruses live in different places during the year. In the summer, **the ice melts** in the southern Arctic. So the walruses head north. The air is cooler there. And ice is still on the water. They often **ride** on chunks of ice to get there. When fall comes, there is ice once again in the south. So the walruses go back. Moving from **place to place** like this is called **migration.**

This walrus is floating on a chunk of ice.

Walruses live on ice and in very cold water. They have almost no hair on their body to act **as a blanket.** So they need a way to stay warm. This is what their **blubber** is for. Walruses have a **thick layer** of fat under their skin that holds in body heat. It protects them from the cold. Seals and whales have blubber, too.

Cold water makes a walrus's skin turn white. After being in the sun, it turns brown again.

5 ▸ What Do Walruses Eat?

Walruses feed on many different kinds of animals. Sometimes they look for animals that live **in the mud** on the ocean floor. Clams and starfish are two of their favorites. But really hungry walruses **hunt seals.**

This walrus is diving for food in the cold Arctic water.

I think I'm in the wrong place at the wrong time!

Walruses live together in groups called **herds.** At certain times of the year, thousands of walruses get together. Round Island is one place that is famous for its herds. In fact, some of the older walruses never leave. They stay all year long, **resting in the sun.**

Walruses tell each other how they are feeling by touching, smelling, and making sounds. They might **grunt,** snort, bark, or even growl!

These walruses are using each other as pillows at Round Island, Alaska.

Male walruses, or **bulls,** are able to make a special noise under the water. It sounds a lot like a bell ringing. The females, or **cows,** can't make this noise. When bulls make this sound, they are said to be "**pinging.**" Pinging bulls might be sending out a warning to others to **stay away.** Or they might be trying to attract females.

This young walrus is
exploring under the water.

A cow usually has just one baby, or **calf,** at a time. The calf needs its mother for everything. The cow takes care of her calf for a long time. She protects it and feeds it milk from her body. The calf can live on its own when it is about two years old. By this time, it has learned how to find food.

This walrus cow and her calf live in the Canadian Arctic.

8 Do Walruses Have Enemies?

Walruses don't have many enemies. But the ones they do have are **very dangerous.** Killer whales sometimes catch walruses that are swimming in the water. They are bigger, **stronger,** and faster than the walrus. So even the tusks of the walrus can't help save it from this enemy. **Polar bears** look for small walruses that are out of the water. A calf resting on the shore is an easy catch.

This walrus calf stays safe by resting on its mother's back.

Those tusks don't scare me!

People living in some parts of the far north **hunt and kill** walruses. But they use every part of the body for things they need. They eat the meat. They use the skin to build boats. They also **make tools** out of the tusks and bones.

This long-tusked male lives in a protected area near Round Island, Alaska.

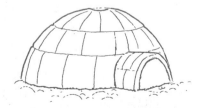

In the past, people killed many walruses just for their **ivory** tusks. The ivory was sold and made into such things as **jewelry.** So many were killed that their future was in danger.

But **people have helped** to save the walruses. Laws have been passed to protect them. The number of walruses has grown. So they are safe for now. Today, walruses can still be found in the cold waters of the Arctic.

This walrus lives in a New York aquarium.

Glossary

blubber a thick layer of fat under the skin of sea mammals

bulls male walruses

calf a baby walrus

cows female walruses

herds groups of animals that live together

ivory a hard substance that makes up an animal's tusks

mammals animals with hair or fur that feed their babies milk from their bodies

migration moving from one place to another

pinnipeds sea mammals that have flippers instead of arms or legs

tusks large teeth that grow out of an animal's mouth